What is the Incarnation?

Basics of the Faith

Sean Michael Lucas, Series Editor

What Is the Incarnation?

William B. Evans

P U B L I S H I N G

P.O. BOX 817 • PHILLIPSBURG • NEW JERSEY 08865-0817

ISBN: 978-1-59638-829-1 (pbk)
ISBN: 978-59638-830-7 (ePub)
ISBN: 978-1-59638-831-4 (Mobi)

Page design by Tobias Design

Printed in the United States of America

Library of Congress Cataloging-in-Publication Data

Evans, William B.
  What is the Incarnation? / William B. Evans.
     pages cm. -- (Basics of the faith)
  Includes bibliographical references.
  ISBN 978-1-59638-829-1 (pbk.)
  1. Jesus Christ--Person and offices. 2. Incarnation. I. Title.
  BT203.E93 2013
  232'.1--dc23
                              2013023451

■ **This booklet** is an introduction to Christology (the doctrine of the person of Christ)—a topic that lies at the center of Christian faith. As we will soon see, there is much to think about here, but at the outset a crucial point needs to be made. Although there are issues of Christology that continue to perplex and fascinate theologians, the doctrine of the incarnation is first and foremost a matter of doxology rather than an intellectual puzzle. It is something that should cause us to marvel at the matchless grace of God and to respond to that grace with worship and praise. After all, the second person of the Trinity has come to us in human form to save helpless sinners, to accomplish salvation for us, to unite us with himself, and so to raise us up into fellowship and communion with God. Even as our faith seeks understanding on this issue, may we be driven to worship and adore the God who has created us for himself, who has revealed himself to us in his written and incarnate Word, and who has by the work of that incarnate Word redeemed a people for himself.[1]

Anyone who desires to be a Christian must answer two vital questions. The first is this: who is Jesus Christ? The second follows quickly upon the first: what has Christ done for me so that I may be saved? As we shall see, our explorations here will focus on the first question, but we must touch on the second as well.

According to the great confessional tradition of the church, in dependence upon Scripture we affirm that Christ is both truly God (*vere deus*) and truly human (*vere homo*) and that these two natures nevertheless comprise one divine-human person. Echoing the Council of Chalcedon (A.D. 451), the Westminster Confession of Faith declares "that two whole, perfect, and distinct natures, the Godhead and the manhood, were inseparably joined together in one person, without conversion, composition, or confusion. Which person is very God and very man, yet one Christ, the only Mediator between God and man."[2] Admittedly, this is the careful language of technical theology, but here the Westminster divines express truth that is of momentous, indeed essential, practical importance. Thus we must be careful not to dismiss these somewhat technical discussions of the person of Christ as irrelevant to the life and health of the church, or as of little consequence for our Christian lives.

SOME PRELIMINARY COMMENTS

As we suggested above, we cannot ultimately separate the doctrine of Christ's person from the doctrine of his work. They go together, because Jesus was perfectly fitted for the work he came to do. This strong connection of person and work is evident in the two most influential theological arguments for the full deity of Christ from the early and medieval church periods. The first is by Athanasius of Alexandria (c. 296–373), that stalwart hero of the faith who did more to defeat the Arian heresy (which denied the deity of Christ) than any other. He wrote in his treatise "On the Incarnation":

> The reason of his bodily appearing; that it was in the power of none other to turn the corruptible to incorruption, except the Saviour himself, that had at the beginning also made all things out of naught; and that none other could create anew the likeness of God's image for men, save the image of the Father; that none other could render the mortal immortal, save our Lord Jesus Christ, who is the very life; and that

none other could teach men of the Father, and destroy the worship of idols, save the Word, that orders all things and is alone the true only begotten Son of the Father.[3]

Here the great bishop of Alexandria argues that sin has decisively separated humanity from God who is the source of life and immortality, that only God himself can fix the situation, and that Christ therefore must be fully God. Note also that Athanasius is pointing us to a particular aspect of Christ's saving work—his transforming work *in us*.

The second great argument regarding the person of Christ was presented by that remarkable medieval theologian Anselm of Canterbury (c. 1033–1109). In his treatise entitled *Cur Deus Homo* (*Why the God-Man*), the great archbishop of Canterbury notes that human sin has resulted in alienation because God's infinite honor has been offended and a proper satisfaction must be offered. Furthermore, only God can offer such infinite satisfaction and only man should offer satisfaction, and so the one offering such satisfaction must be the God-man. Anselm's formulation here is worth quoting in full:

> For God will not do it, because he does not owe it, and man will not do it, because he cannot. Therefore, for the God-Man to do this, the person who is to make this satisfaction must be both perfect God and perfect man, because none but true God can make it, and none but true man owes it. Thus, while it is necessary to find a God-Man in whom the integrity of both natures is preserved, it is no less necessary for these two complete natures to meet in one person—just as body and rational soul meet in one man—for otherwise the same person could not be perfect God and perfect man.[4]

Here we see that Anselm is focusing particularly on the question of what Christ does *for us*. To rephrase the matter in more familiar terms, we recognize that God is just and that human sin must be punished. After all, as the apostle Paul teaches, "the wages of sin is death" (Rom. 6:23). The only way for sinners to be redeemed from this penalty of eternal death is for a perfect sacrifice to be offered, and Jesus as the God-man is this perfect and all-sufficient sacrifice for sin on our behalf as he took upon himself the penalty that we deserve. Thus Christians have rightly sensed that Jesus Christ must be exactly who the Bible says he is—God and man in a single person—in order that he might both reconcile us to God and transform us into the people God wants us to be.

This doctrine of the person of Christ is also inevitably connected with other crucial doctrines of the faith. Because Christ is fully God and fully human, it is closely related to what theologians call "theology proper" (the doctrine of God) and to theological anthropology (the doctrine of humanity). History demonstrates that it is particularly connected to our understanding of humanity in its sinful and fallen condition. Some have argued that the human condition is not grave, and that all we need is a bit of education and encouragement to do what is right. In other words, a modest savior will do. Such people often deny that Christ is God and view him as little more than a human teacher and example of moral truth.[5] On the other hand, if the human condition in sin is not only grave but completely beyond our capacity to rectify it, if we are truly dead in trespasses and sins, then we need a grand and mighty Savior, one who is no less than God himself. In addition, the doctrine of the incarnation is related to our doctrine of salvation, for all of salvation comes to us through our spiritual union with Christ (see Eph. 1:3–14), and he is the mediator between God and human beings (1 Tim. 2:5). Finally, it is related to ecclesiology, or the doctrine of the church, for the church is the body of Christ (see Rom. 12:3–8; 1 Cor. 12:12–31). Thus we have ample reason and incentive to get this doctrine of the person of Christ right.

One final comment needs to be made. We must not suppose that we can rationally explain the incarnation, and it is with good reason that Christians have long spoken of the "mystery" of the incarnation. As we will see later in this booklet, this fact has been a stumbling block for some, but we should not be surprised in the least that there is mystery involved here. If the incarnation—the union of infinite deity and finite humanity in a single person—is a reality, then we should not expect fully to comprehend this fact. It is by definition a unique event, and thus we ought not to use the categories of our ordinary experience as arguments against it. As the late Scottish theologian Thomas F. Torrance notes,

> We cannot compare the fact of Christ with other facts, nor can we deduce the fact of Christ from our knowledge of other facts. The fact of Christ comes breaking into the continuity of our human knowledge as an utterly distinctive and unique fact, which we cannot understand in terms of other facts, which we cannot reduce to what we already know. It is a new and unique fact without analogy anywhere in human experience or knowledge.[6]

At the same time, we should also recognize that the incarnation is a mystery with great explanatory power, for the New Testament everywhere presupposes it and makes little sense without it. Theologian J. I. Packer writes,

> Once we grant that Jesus was divine, it becomes unreasonable to find difficulty in any of this [i.e., other teachings of the New Testament]; it is all of a piece and hangs together completely. The Incarnation is in itself an unfathomable mystery, but it makes sense of everything else that the New Testament contains.[7]

THE BIBLICAL WITNESS TO THE PERSON OF CHRIST

As many are aware, terms such as *Trinity* and *incarnation* are not found in Scripture. They are, however, useful and appropriate terms for describing what the Bible teaches about God and Christ. In fact, the biblical witness to the person of Christ is vast and resounding, and Christians need feel no embarrassment on this issue when they speak with those who deny that Christ is God. That being said, we can only begin to explore this matter here.

The Old Testament

The Old Testament materials, as we might imagine in the pagan and polytheistic context of the ancient Near East, are particularly focused on the oneness of the true God over against the many gods of the nations. Even so, there are striking indications that the promised Messiah was to be both human and divine. In fulfillment of the Davidic covenant he was to be the son of David who will reign on the throne of David forever (see Isa. 11:1–5). Moreover, the messianic child prophesied by Isaiah will at the same time be called "Wonderful Counselor, Mighty God, Everlasting Father, Prince of Peace" (see Isa. 9:6–7). In addition, the so-called "royal psalms" sometimes ascribe divine identity and qualities to the Davidic kings, and such psalms were rightly interpreted as messianic by the Jews of the later Old Testament period (see, e.g., Pss. 2:7; 45:6–7; 110:1). The richness of this Old Testament witness is such that the New Testament writers had much to work with when the Messiah finally came.

The New Testament

The New Testament materials are, as we would expect, much more extensive and complex. The Synoptic Gospels (Matthew, Mark, and Luke) emphasize in various ways that Jesus was fully human. For example, Matthew's gospel begins by affirming that Jesus is the "son of David" and the "son of Abraham." Human genealogies of Jesus are found in Matthew and Luke (see Matt. 1:2–17; Luke 3:23–38), and Luke's gospel emphasizes that Jesus underwent a normal human process of development, that he "increased in wisdom and in stature and in favor with God and man" (Luke 2:52). At the same time, while the writers of the Synoptic Gospels do not expressly speak of Jesus as "God," they everywhere assume his deity by ascribing divine functions to Jesus. For example, Jesus has the power to forgive sins (see Matt. 9:2–6). He is Lord of the Sabbath (Mark 2:23–27). He possesses a unique knowledge of God the Father (Matt. 11:27). He will come in glory to judge the nations and establish the eternal kingdom of God (Matt. 25:31–32), and after the resurrection he declares that "all authority in heaven and on earth has been given to me" (Matt. 28:18). All this makes little sense if Christ is not God as well as man.

Of the four gospels it is John's that provides the most explicit witness to the deity of Christ. The opening prologue is particularly striking in that it provides important building blocks for the doctrine of the Trinity by speaking of the relationship between the divine Word and God as one of both identity and differentiation: "In the beginning was the Word (Greek: *Logos*), and the Word was with God, and the Word was God" (John 1:1). In other words, while there is one God, both the Word and the Father are God, and the Word is distinct from the Father. It goes on to speak of the Word's involvement in the divine act of creation (John 1:3), before triumphantly declaring that "the Word became flesh and dwelt among us, and we have seen his glory, glory as of the only Son from the Father, full of grace and truth" (John 1:14). Quite a number of Jesus' statements in this gospel must finally be interpreted as claims to deity. He expressly claims to be one with the Father (John 10:30–39), and particularly striking are the various "I am" sayings by Jesus where he identifies himself with the divine name *I AM* in the Old Testament (see, e.g., John 6:20; 8:12, 57–59; 11:25; cf. Ex. 3:13–14). Finally, at the close of this gospel Jesus' identity as God is recognized by "Doubting Thomas" (John 20:28). At the same time, John's gospel also presents Jesus as fully human—he is subject to human physical limitations such as fatigue, hunger, and thirst (John 4:6–8; 19:28), and his sorrow at the grave of his dear friend Lazarus demonstrates that Jesus had a genuinely human emotional life (John 11:33–35).

The Pauline epistles contain two passages that are best translated as direct ascriptions of deity to Christ (Rom. 9:5; Titus 2:13). Just as important, the Epistles of the New Testament provide further evidence that the incarnation is a foundational assumption of the New Testament writers. For example, the Greek word *kurios* ("Lord") is persistently used of Christ, and this very word was used in the Greek version of the Old Testament to translate the Hebrew divine name *Yahweh*. Old Testament passages speaking of Yahweh are applied to Christ (see Isa. 45:23; cf. Rom. 14:9–11). There are statements that say in so many words that what God is, Christ is (see Phil. 2:6; Col. 1:19; 2:9). Similar sentiments are expressed by the author of the book of Hebrews, for whom Christ "is the radiance of the glory of God and the exact imprint of his nature, and he upholds the universe by the word of his power" (Heb. 1:3). At the same time, the apostle Paul emphasizes that Christ was fully human—that he suffered on the cross and died for our sins. The author of Hebrews also strongly affirms the full humanity of Christ and sees it as essential to his high priestly work: "Therefore he had to be made like his brothers in every respect, so that he might become a merciful and faithful high priest in the service of God, to make propitiation for the sins of the people" (Heb. 2:17).

THE CHURCH EXPLORES THE MYSTERY OF THE INCARNATION

As we saw in the brief survey above, Scripture provides ample and compelling witness to both the true deity and the true humanity of Christ. But how is the scriptural data to be understood? The Bible affirms that Jesus is both God and man, and it also presents him as an integrated personality, but how can finite humanity and infinite deity coexist in a single person? In fact, it took the church several centuries to sort through the various possibilities in order to arrive at a stable and authoritative formulation of the matter. As someone has said, the wheels of theology grind slowly, but they grind exceedingly finely, and the development of the church's understanding of the incarnation is a case in point.

The process whereby the church worked through these issues can be helpfully presented in terms of the six major heresies associated with the person of Christ that arose in the early church—two having to do with the integrity of his deity, two with the integrity of his humanity, and two with the relationship between the deity and the humanity.[8] In each instance the church quickly came to realize that these views did not measure up to what Scripture teaches.

Ebionism

An early misunderstanding of the incarnation is known as Ebionism. The term "Ebionite" means "poor," and what we know of the Ebionites comes to us secondhand from the writings of the church fathers. Apparently, the Ebionites were poor Jewish people who accepted Jesus as the Messiah but who had difficulty reconciling the doctrine of the incarnation with their Jewish monotheism. Thus they viewed Jesus as a mere man who was indwelt by the Spirit of God and "adopted" as the "Son of God" at his baptism. Thus they would affirm that God was in Christ, but not that Christ was God, and their view of Jesus was basically that of a great prophet. But such teaching obviously did not do justice to the richness of what Scripture teaches about Christ. Unfortunately, similar teachings are popular in some circles today.

Docetism

A second heresy, known as "Docetism" (from the Greek word *dokein*, "to seem"), admitted that Jesus was in some sense a divine being, but it denied his essential humanity. It was especially popular among the Gnostics, who believed in salvation by secret knowledge provided by a mediator from the spiritual realm, and whose dualistic understanding of reality viewed the material realm as evil.[9] If Jesus was the gnostic mediator/messenger who had come from the spiritual realm in order to bring saving knowledge, then they supposed that he could not have been compromised by material existence, and so they viewed his humanity as phantasmal. He only "seemed" to be human. Such ideas were clearly on the scene by the early second century, and the apostle John may well be referring to this error when he speaks of those who deny "that Jesus Christ has come in the flesh" (1 John 4:2).

Arianism

In the early fourth century a priest in Alexandria, Egypt, by the name of Arius taught that the Word or Logos was but the highest of the creatures, that the Logos had a beginning, and that the Logos could have fallen into sin. In essence, Arius viewed Christ as a lesser "god" but not as God. This teaching, of course, constituted a decisive repudiation of the deity of Christ, and the great Athanasius of Alexandria opposed it, not only on the grounds that it was contrary to Scripture, but also that it made salvation impossible. Such a Christ, Athanasius cogently argued, cannot save us, and his arguments prevailed at the Council of Nicaea (A.D. 325) and the Council of Constantinople (A.D. 381). Unfortunately, however, such ideas are still with us, for the teachings of the contemporary Jehovah's Witnesses closely resemble this ancient heresy of Arianism.[10]

Apollinarianism

Later in the fourth century, a bishop of Laodicea (an ancient city in the western portion of what is now modern Turkey) named Apollinaris, who apparently viewed the human mind as inherently sinful, sought to safeguard the psychological integrity of Christ by having the Logos take the place of the human mind and soul as the rational principle of Christ's person. This, of course, was a denial of the full humanity of Christ, and the church fathers opposed Apollinaris, not only because his teachings were contrary to Scripture, but also because it made salvation impossible. If we are to be saved as complete human beings—body and soul—they argued, Christ must therefore have assumed, or taken to himself, a complete humanity. "What is not assumed," they rightly declared, "is not saved." Thus it was that Apollinarianism was condemned at the Council of Constantinople in A.D. 381. While these doctrinal disputes were no doubt unpleasant, they also illustrate the way that the challenge of heresy can cause the church to reflect more deeply and adequately on what Scripture teaches.

Nestorianism

With the integrity of both the deity and the humanity of Christ decisively affirmed by the Council of Constantinople, attention soon turned to the question of how the deity and humanity relate to one another in the context of a single, integrated divine-human person. From around A.D. 430 to 451 a "christological controversy" raged. The historical details of this period are too complicated to explore here, but we gain an appreciation of the issues involved by examining the two chief heresies, which in turn gave rise to the great christological settlement of the Council of Chalcedon in A.D. 451.

The Nestorian heresy is named after Nestorius, who briefly served as the bishop of Constantinople from A.D. 428–31. Nestorius affirmed the integrity of the divine and human natures, but he was unclear about the unity of the person of Christ. He spoke of the deity and humanity as each having its own subsistence or "hypostasis," and as "conjoined" rather than united. This understandably seemed to many to smack of two separate persons squeezed together without any real union of the two. In short, the Jesus of Nestorius seemed to be schizoid, with two distinct persons inhabiting a single body. How could such an odd being accomplish redemption and save us? Not surprisingly, the views of Nestorius were quickly rejected by the Council of Ephesus in A.D. 431, and Nestorius himself was exiled to a monastery.

Eutychianism

But almost immediately the opposite error arose. The Eutychian heresy, named after a monk of Constantinople named Eutyches, spoke of Christ as having one divine-human nature, and Eutyches seems to have taught that the humanity of Christ is qualitatively different from ours. In other words, Eutyches so closely related the deity and the humanity of Christ that the infinite deity seemed to swallow up the finite humanity, such that Christ was no longer like us in every way except for sin. Again the reaction was swift, for most Christians realized that Christ's oneness with the humanity he came to save is of crucial importance. Eutychianism threatened the very possibility of salvation.

The Council of Chalcedon

All this brings us to one of the great watersheds in early church history—the Fourth Ecumenical Council, which was held at Chalcedon in A.D. 451. At this meeting the views of Eutyches were condemned, and the Council wrote a statement that carefully expressed the consensus that had emerged after several centuries of christological discussion. Three points need to be noted regarding this Chalcedonian Christology. First, against Eutyches, the Council affirmed that Christ possesses two natures—a divine nature and a human nature. In this way, the Council underscored that Christ is fully God and at the same time fully human. Second, against Nestorius the Council affirmed that these two natures exist in hypostatic union. That is, the two natures form one "subsistence" or "person." In this way the Council safeguarded the unity of the person. Third, the Council described this relationship of the divine and the human in Christ by using primarily negative terminology ("without confusion, without change, without division, without separation"). That is, the Council did not presume to define it exhaustively or to explain it. After all, the theologians and churchmen present knew full well that they were dealing with a divine and holy mystery. All this is quite evident in this famous language from the decree of the Council, according to which Christ is

> to be acknowledged in two natures, without confusion, without change, without division, without separation; the distinction of natures being in no way abolished because of the union, but rather the characteristic property of each nature being preserved, and concurring into one Person and one subsistence (*hypostasis*), not as if Christ were parted or divided into two persons, but one and the same Son and only-begotten God, Word, Lord Jesus Christ; even as the prophets from the beginning spoke concerning him, and our Lord Jesus Christ instructed us, and the Creed of the Fathers has handed down to us.[11]

The Council of Chalcedon was a watershed event, but it was certainly not the end of christological debate in the early church period. For example, there were some who disagreed with the results of Chalcedon and who continued to speak of Christ as one divine-human nature. Thus there are Monophysite ("one-nature") churches that persist down to the present day (such as the Coptic and Armenian churches in the Middle East). In addition, there were discussions as to whether Christ had one will or two. This Monothelite ("one will") controversy was settled by the Third Council of Constantinople in A.D. 680–81, which decided that Christ possesses both a divine and a human will (because a human being without a human will is obviously incomplete) but that the two are in perfect harmony.

Theologians after Chalcedon such as Leontius of Byzantium (who died c. A.D. 543) and John of Damascus (A.D. 675–749) continued to ponder the relationship between the divine and the human. In order further to safeguard the unity of the person of Christ, they argued that the humanity of Christ does not have its own independent hypostasis (*anhypostasia*) but that it has its hypostasis or subsistence in the Logos (*enhypostasia*). While such ideas may seem to us rather abstract, they serve to underscore that the divine Logos did not happen upon a previously existing human being and take it over. Seen in this light, these ideas are useful and are defended by theologians even today.

Post-Enlightenment Criticism of the Incarnation

The Council of Chalcedon marks a decisive point in the church's reflection on the incarnation, and it has long served as a doctrinal benchmark for Christians in both the East and the West. But with the Enlightenment (c. 1650–1800) this began to change. This was the "Age of Reason," and extraordinary emphasis was placed upon the alleged adequacy and autonomy of human reason. That is, many came to believe that human reason is adequate to discover all truth, that reason is the highest authority, and that it need answer to no other standard (such as divine revelation in Scripture).

Obviously such ideas had implications for how Jesus Christ was viewed, and these are evident in at least two ways. First, the emphasis upon human reason as the final judge of all truth left little room for divine mystery, and increasingly the doctrine of the incarnation was viewed as irrational or worse. Second, the Enlightenment was profoundly anthropocentric, and this man-centered mindset increasingly meant that when people did think about Jesus they began with the humanity of Christ as a given, and only then did they ask about his divinity. That is to say, in contrast to much of the thinking of the early and medieval church, which started christological reflection with the deity and then sought to understand how Christ's humanity fit in with that divine reality (a "Christology from above"), post-Enlightenment theology has often begun with the humanity and sought to work upward (a "Christology from below"). For example, some became convinced that the attributes of infinite deity simply were incompatible with finite humanity, and particularly with finite human consciousness. The net result of all this was that the traditional Christian doctrine of the deity of Christ came to be seen by some as implausible, and for these reasons the two-natures doctrine of Chalcedon was subjected to considerable criticism in the nineteenth and twentieth centuries.

A variety of alternatives to Chalcedon have been suggested in the modern period, and while space precludes a detailed discussion here, we can briefly mention two such proposals by way of example. First, the so-called "Kenotic Christologies" of the nineteenth and early twentieth centuries sought to explain the incarnation by suggesting that the Son of God "emptied himself" of some or all of the divine attributes when he became man. Proponents of this view appealed to Philippians 2:7, where the apostle Paul says that Christ "emptied himself, taking the form of a servant" (RSV). Thus some have argued for a *kenosis* of the divine Son (a noun related to the Greek verb meaning "to empty"). Of course, in this passage Paul does not say that Christ emptied himself of anything in particular, or that he discarded his divine attributes. In fact, the transfiguration narratives in the three

Synoptic Gospels suggest that Jesus' divine attributes were, as Calvin argued, "hidden" rather than relinquished. Rather, the emphasis here is on the way that he assumed a lowly human mode of existence in the incarnation, and so the scriptural basis for such Kenotic Christologies is slim. As is often pointed out, such kenotic approaches subvert both the doctrine of divine immutability (changelessness) and the doctrine of the incarnation itself, in that they assume that the second person of the Trinity could become human only by ceasing in some sense to be God.[12]

Second, there is the more recent theory of "retroactive constitution" proposed by the contemporary German theologian Wolfhart Pannenberg. He explicitly rejects the two-natures doctrine of Chalcedon, but still wants to speak of Christ as God, and so Pannenberg argues that the unity of God and man in Christ must be seen in light of the resurrection event. In fact, it is retroactively constituted by Christ's resurrection on Easter morning. Pannenberg writes, "But through his resurrection it is decided, not only so far as our knowledge is concerned, but with respect to reality, that Jesus is one with God and retroactively that he was also already one with God previously."[13] Obviously this theory not only stands in tension with the biblical passages speaking of the preexistence of the Logos (John 1:1–4, 14; Phil. 2:5–11), but it is also heavily dependent upon some rather arcane philosophical presuppositions. For these reasons Pannenberg's theory has elicited more curiosity than acceptance. Thus, at the end of the day these modern alternatives to Chalcedon are a good deal less convincing than the theory they propose to replace.

IS THERE A DISTINCTIVELY REFORMED CHRISTOLOGY?

Having examined the church's reflection on the person of Christ more broadly, another question emerges: is there a distinctively Reformed approach to the person of Christ? The short answer to this question is a decisive no. John Calvin staunchly defended the creedal doctrine of the person of Christ, for he believed that the early ecumenical councils of the church were simply stating what Scripture teaches. Note how Calvin carefully preserves the primacy of Scripture while at the same time giving appropriate deference to decisions of the Councils:

> Thus councils would come to have the majesty that is their due; yet in the meantime Scripture would stand out in the higher place, with everything subject to its standard. In this way, we willingly embrace and reverence as holy the early councils, such as those of Nicaea, Constantinople, Ephesus I, Chalcedon, and the like, which were concerned with refuting errors—in so far as they relate to the teachings of faith. For they contain nothing but the pure and genuine exposition of Scripture, which the holy fathers applied with spiritual prudence to crush the enemies of religion who had then arisen.[14]

And Calvin is not alone, for more recent conservative Reformed theologians such as Charles Hodge, B. B. Warfield, Herman Bavinck, Louis Berkhof, and John Murray have likewise been staunch defenders of the two-natures doctrine of Chalcedon.[15] Witness this striking affirmation from the great Old Princetonian B. B. Warfield:

> That is to say, the doctrine of the Two Natures of Christ is not merely the synthesis of the teaching of the New Testament, but the conception which underlies every one of the New Testament writings severally; it is not only the teaching of the New Testament as a whole but of the whole of the New Testament, part by part. Historically, this means that not only has the doctrine of the Two Natures been the invariable

presupposition of the whole teaching of the church from the apostolic age down, but all the teaching of the apostolic age rests on it as its universal presupposition.[16]

All that being said, are there nevertheless distinctive christological emphases among Reformed theologians? Here the answer is a qualified yes, and it is worthwhile to look at this question more carefully. Earlier we referred to the Nestorian and Eutychian heresies (see pp. 15–16). These were, in fact, more radical examples of broader christological approaches that we associate with the ancient cities of Alexandria in Egypt and Antioch in Syria.[17] In brief, as Christians sought to understand how Christ can be both God and man and yet a single person, there were those who emphasized the unity of the person of Christ (the school of Alexandria) and those who stressed the integrity of the two natures and sought to ensure that the incarnate humanity was not swallowed up by the deity (the school of Antioch). Of course, both concerns are legitimate, but when pushed to extremes they can lead to problems. For example, Nestorianism can be viewed as the Antiochian approach pushed too far, and Eutychianism as the Alexandrian run amok. As we have seen, the Council of Chalcedon sought to avoid both extremes.

In its affirmations of Chalcedon, the Reformed tradition has often tilted slightly toward the concerns of Antioch. We can better grasp this fact by means of a comparison with the Lutheran tradition, which, conversely, tilts toward Alexandria. The Lutheran tradition teaches that the divine and human natures of Christ are so closely associated that there is a real "communication of attributes" such that Christ's incarnate humanity has become ubiquitous (or "present everywhere"). This in turn provides a basis for the Lutheran doctrine of the presence of Christ in the Lord's Supper (known as "consubstantiation"), which holds that Christ's body and blood are locally and physically present "in, with, and under" the elements of bread and wine.[18] For Calvin and the Reformed tradition, however, such thinking is dangerous in that it implies that Christ's humanity is qualitatively different from ours, and so Calvin insists that Christ's humanity is finite, that it remains in heaven, and that the Lutheran doctrine of ubiquity is to be rejected. This does not mean, however, that Calvin rejected the true presence of Christ in the Lord's Supper. We receive the whole Christ, humanity included, as we are lifted up by the power of the Holy Spirit to commune with him in heaven.[19]

This leads us directly to a related matter (a corollary, in fact, of Calvin's rejection of ubiquity) that is often considered a Reformed distinctive—the doctrine of the *extra Calvinisticum*, or the "Calvinistic extra" (a term coined by the Lutherans). In opposing the Lutheran doctrine of ubiquity, and others such as Menno Simons (whose doctrine of the "celestial flesh" of Christ was essentially Monophysite), Calvin maintained that the presence of the infinite Logos is not circumscribed by the incarnate humanity of Christ. In other words, even while Christ hung on the cross, he was ruling over the cosmos! Witness this striking passage from Calvin:

> They thrust upon us as something absurd the fact that if the Word of God became flesh, then he was confined within the narrow prison of an earthly body. This is mere impudence! For even if the Word in his immeasurable essence united with the nature of man into one person, we do not imagine that he was confined therein. Here is something marvelous: The Son of God descended from heaven in such a way that, without leaving heaven, he willed to be borne in the virgin's womb, to go about on the earth, and to hang upon the cross; yet he continually filled the world even as he had done from the beginning![20]

Three important points need to be noted regarding this *extra Calvinisticum*. First, it represents a genuinely biblical insight. If

God is infinite, as Scripture clearly teaches, and if humanity is finite, as Scripture again teaches, and if Scripture speaks of cosmic functions of Christ that go beyond the scope of the human such as his providential government of the world (e.g., Col. 1:17), then this doctrinal insight is well founded. Thus it finds a place in the Heidelberg Catechism (QQ. 47–48). Second, in light of this we should not be surprised to discover that it is by no means a doctrine peculiar to the Reformed. As theologian E. David Willis has demonstrated in his outstanding study of the *extra Calvinisticum*, the concept is found widely in the fathers of the ancient and medieval church, and he suggests therefore that it is perhaps better termed the *"extra Catholicum."*[21] Finally, this doctrinal insight is useful in that it helps us at least begin to think about how infinite deity and finite humanity can coexist in a single person.

WHAT SORT OF HUMANITY DID CHRIST ASSUME?

Since the early nineteenth century there have been persistent debates regarding the sort of humanity that Christ assumed. Was it a perfected humanity or was it humanity tainted by the effects of sin, a "fallen humanity"? This issue initially came to the fore because of an early nineteenth-century Scottish minister named Edward Irving, who was deposed from the Church of Scotland in 1833 for teaching that Christ assumed a fallen human nature. Similar ideas were propounded later in the nineteenth century by the American Mercersburg theologian John W. Nevin, and most recently and insistently by Thomas F. Torrance.[22] Torrance contends that "the Incarnation is to be understood as the coming of God to take upon himself our fallen human nature, our actual human existence laden with sin and guilt, our humanity diseased in mind and soul in its estrangement or alienation from the Creator."[23] Torrance goes on to insist that this "sinful flesh" or "fallen humanity" of Christ is then sanctified and transformed by its incarnational union with the Logos.[24]

Here some points of clarification need to be noted. First, we must understand that in speaking of the sinful humanity of Christ such theologians are not questioning the actual sinlessness of Christ. Second, they are seeking to emphasize the solidarity of Christ with those he came to save. Third, they stress that in a concrete sense our broken humanity has been healed in Christ and thus that all of salvation is to be found in him.

That being said, some further comments are in order. Certainly Jesus did come to live in a fallen world. He was subject to temptation, suffering, and death. His triumph over temptation was real. He was made "perfect through suffering" (Heb. 2:10), and he "learned obedience through what he suffered" (Heb. 5:8). In other words, Scripture does indeed emphasize that Christ was "made like his brothers in every respect" (Heb. 2:17), and that as the second Adam he triumphed where the first Adam failed (see Rom. 5:12–21). However, we should also recognize that this language about the "sinful" or "fallen" humanity of Christ is provocative and ultimately unhelpful. When many people hear it, they reflexively think that the sinlessness of Christ is at least implicitly being denied, and that is reason enough for us to avoid this language. Finally, theologian Bruce McCormack has shown that the Reformed tradition has more generally maintained that the sanctification of Christ's human nature takes place by the work of the Holy Spirit and not through the hypostatic union of Christ's humanity with the Logos (see, e.g., Westminster Confession of Faith, 8.3).[25]

THE SECOND COMMANDMENT AND PICTURES OF JESUS

A practical question having to do with the doctrine of the incarnation has also arisen in the Reformed tradition. The second commandment prohibits the making of "a carved image, or any likeness of anything that is in heaven above, or that is in the earth beneath, or that is in the water under the earth" (Ex. 20:4), and the Westminster Larger Catechism elaborates on this principle by forbidding "the making any representation of God, of all or of any of the three persons, either inwardly in our mind, or outwardly in any kind of image or likeness of any creature whatsoever" (Westminster Larger Catechism, Q. 109). Understandably, people often ask whether this applies to pictorial representations of Jesus. Indeed, congregations have been torn by controversies over stained-glass depictions of Jesus as the Good Shepherd in sanctuaries and the use of pictures of Jesus in children's Sunday school materials.

In context, this biblical prohibition is clearly directed against all forms of idolatry (see Ex. 20:5). Scripture emphasizes the spirituality and invisibility of God (see John 4:24; Col. 1:15; 1 Tim. 1:17; 6:16), and the biblical writers knew full well that any pictorial representation of God inevitably distorts this spirituality of God. Thus the danger of idolatry is very real, and, against the Greek and Roman Catholic traditions with their extensive use of icons and statues of Jesus, the Reformed tradition has been especially careful on this point. Here we do well to recall Calvin's warning "that man's nature, so to speak, is a perpetual factory of idols."[26]

All that being said, we must also remember that Jesus is not simply God. He is the God-man, the Word made flesh. His humanity was real—his body was visible and tangible—and if photographic or video technology had been available in the first century A.D. we might well have pictures of Jesus available to us. Furthermore, some of the scriptural passages that speak of the invisibility of God at the same time teach that this visible Christ has made God known to us, that as the apostle Paul teaches, "He is the image of the invisible God" (Col. 1:15; cf. John 1:14–18). And if Christ is indeed the preeminent and divinely authorized "image" of God,[27] then the Old Testament prohibition of visual portrayals of God must be interpreted in light of the Christ event. All this suggests that the danger here is not so much the simple violation of the second commandment. Certainly pictures of Jesus can be helpful in teaching children the stories of the Gospels, and we can scarcely be expected to read the gospel accounts without forming a mental image of the events in our minds.

But are there dangers to be concerned about here? Indeed there are! One of the lessons of history is that Christians have tended to fashion views and images of Jesus that are congenial to themselves. Thus Jesus often becomes the exemplar of whatever human beings at a particular time happen to value or admire rather than the Jesus of Scripture. Here we think, for example, of those infamous "Aryan Jesus" paintings portraying Jesus as tall, blond, and blue-eyed, or of what Stephen J. Nichols has called the "Gentle Jesus, Meek and Mild" of sentimental Victorian culture, or of the political revolutionary Jesus of Marxist-influenced liberation theology.[28] The list of such distortions is nearly endless. Particularly egregious was the Jesus-as-merely-human-moral-teacher-and-example of nineteenth-century German Protestant liberals such as Adolph von Harnack, which prompted the English Roman Catholic theologian George Tyrrell in 1909 to quip, "The Christ that Harnack sees, looking back through nineteen centuries of Catholic darkness, is only the reflection of a Liberal Protestant face, seen at the bottom of a deep well."[29]

For these reasons we should be cautious, not only about visual pictures of Jesus, but also about the conceptual portrayals of him that we create for ourselves. We must constantly return to Scripture in order to correct our "vision" on this matter. After all, in the providence of God we have no visible images of the historical Jesus available to us. In fact, if we want a visible representation of Jesus, Scripture encourages us to find it in other Christians, especially other Christians in need (see Matt. 25:34–40; Acts 9:5).

THE ETERNAL INCARNATION

It is apparent from Scripture that the incarnation is a permanent condition for the second person of the Trinity. The author of the epistle to the Hebrews declares, "Jesus Christ is the same yesterday and today and forever" (Heb. 13:8). As the apostle Paul teaches, we are eternally saved by being spiritually united with Christ, the principle of our own resurrections is to be found in his resurrection, and all this is "so that in the coming ages he might show the immeasurable riches of his grace in kindness toward us in Christ Jesus" (Eph. 2:7; cf. 1 Thess. 4:17). In other words, in Jesus Christ deity and humanity are forever united in a single divine-human person. God himself has chosen to live with us as part of the human community . . . forever! In Christ we have God's final affirmation of human worth and dignity and his eternal commitment in love to us as human beings. This is remarkable and cause for wonder. May we grow in our love for Christ and in our appreciation of his incarnation as we ponder these truths.

A CALL TO DOXOLOGY

In this booklet we have looked at the biblical portrayal of Christ and at the history of the church's encounter with the doctrine of the incarnation. We have also touched on some more technical theological issues that have arisen in the course of the church's discussions of the incarnation. In all of this, however, it is easy to get lost in the details, and perhaps to miss the forest for the trees. We must remember that ultimately the incarnation is about God's purposes to redeem and to live in communion and fellowship with his human creation forever, and the lengths that he will go to do this. We must also remember that the appropriate response to the incarnation is doxology; that is, praise, adoration, and worship.

NOTES

1 Because of these complexities, the doctrine of the incarnation is best approached from the stance of "faith seeking understanding" that we associate especially with Augustine of Hippo and Anselm of Canterbury. Quoting Augustine, Anselm wrote this prayer in his Proslogion: "I acknowledge, O Lord, with thanksgiving, that thou has created this thy image in me, so that, remembering thee, I may think of thee, may love thee. But this image is so effaced and worn away by my faults, it is so obscured by the smoke of my sins, that it cannot do what it was made to do, unless thou renew and reform it. I am not trying, O Lord, to penetrate thy loftiness, for I cannot begin to match my understanding with it, but I desire in some measure to understand thy truth, which my heart believes and loves. For I do not understand in order to believe, but I believe in order to understand. For this too I believe, that 'unless I believe, I shall not understand.'" Anselm of Canterbury, "An Address (Proslogion)," in *A Scholastic Miscellany: Anselm to Ockham*, ed. Eugene R. Fairweather, The Library of Christian Classics, vol. 10 (Philadelphia: Westminster, 1956), 73.

2 Westminster Confession of Faith, 8.2. For the text of the Chalcedonian decree, see J. Stevenson, *Creeds, Councils, and Controversies: Documents Illustrating the History of the Church, AD 337–461*, new edition revised by W. H. C. Frend (London: SPCK, 1989), 350–54.

3 Athanasius, "On the Incarnation," in *Christology of the Later Fathers*, ed. Edward R. Hardy (Philadelphia: Westminster, 1954), 73–74.

4 Anselm of Canterbury, "Why God Became Man," 152.

5 For a devastating criticism of such thinking, see J. Gresham Machen, *Christianity and Liberalism*, new ed. (Grand Rapids: Eerdmans, 2009), 69–98.

6 Thomas F. Torrance, *Incarnation: The Person and Life of Christ*, ed. Robert T. Walker (Downers Grove, IL: InterVarsity Press, 2008), 1.

7 J. I. Packer, *Knowing God*, 20th anniversary ed. (Downers Grove, IL: InterVarsity Press, 1993), 54.

8 The schema and sequence of six major christological heresies presented here draws on Millard Erickson's helpful presentation; see Millard J. Erickson, *Introducing Christian Doctrine*, ed. L. Arnold Hustad (Grand Rapids: Baker, 1992), 212–31. An accessible and reliable guide to the early church discussions is J. N. D. Kelly, *Early Christian Doctrines*, rev. ed. (San Francisco: Harper and Row, 1978). For an extended discussion

of orthodox Christology and heresy, see Harold O. J. Brown, *Heresies: The Image of Christ in the Mirror of Heresy and Orthodoxy from the Apostles to the Present* (Garden City, NY: Doubleday, 1984).

9   On the popularity of gnostic ideas today, see Jay Tolson, "The Gospel Truth: Why Some Old Books Are Stirring Up a New Debate about the Meaning of Jesus," *U.S. News and World Report*, December 18, 2006, 70–72, 75–76, 78–79.

10   For an incisive examination and refutation of the christological views of the Jehovah's Witnesses, see Bruce M. Metzger, "The Jehovah's Witnesses and Jesus Christ: A Biblical and Theological Appraisal," *Theology Today* 10 (April 1953): 65–85.

11   "The Chalcedonian Definition of Faith," in Stevenson, *Creeds, Councils, and Controversies*, 353.

12   See, for example, G. C. Berkouwer, *The Person of Christ*, trans. John Vriend (Grand Rapids: Eerdmans, 1954), 27–31.

13   Wolfhart Pannenberg, *Jesus: God and Man*, 2nd ed., trans. Lewis L. Wilkins and Duane A. Priebe (Philadelphia: Westminster, 1977), 136.

14   John Calvin, *Institutes of the Christian Religion*, 2 vols., ed. John T. McNeill, trans. Ford Lewis Battles (Philadelphia: Westminster, 1960), 4.9.8. For Calvin's treatment of the two-natures doctrine, see *Institutes* 2.12.1–14.8.

15   See Charles Hodge, *Systematic Theology*, 3 vols. (New York: Charles Scribner's Sons, 1872–73), 2:378–454; Benjamin Breckinridge Warfield, "The 'Two Natures' and Recent Christological Speculation," in *The Person and Work of Christ* (Philadelphia: Presbyterian and Reformed, 1950), 211–62; Herman Bavinck, *Reformed Dogmatics*, 4 vols. (Grand Rapids: Baker, 2003–2008), 3:233–319; Louis Berkhof, *Systematic Theology* (Grand Rapids: Eerdmans, 1941), 312–30; and John Murray, *Collected Writings of John Murray*, vol. 2, *Systematic Theology* (Edinburgh: Banner of Truth, 1977), 132–41. Even some Reformed theologians of more liberal persuasion, such as Karl Barth, have (with some qualifications) defended the Chalcedonian formulation. See George Hunsinger, "Karl Barth's Christology: Its Basic Chalcedonian Character," in *Disruptive Grace: Studies in the Theology of Karl Barth* (Grand Rapids: Eerdmans, 2000), 131–47.

16   Warfield, "Recent Christological Speculation," 237.

17   See R. V. Sellers, *Two Ancient Christologies: A Study in the Christological Thought of the Schools of Alexandria and Antioch in the Early History of*

Christian Doctrine (London: SPCK, 1954); and Kelly, *Early Christian Doctrines*, 280–343.

18 See Theodore G. Tappert, trans. and ed., *The Book of Concord: The Confessions of the Evangelical Lutheran Church* (Philadelphia: Fortress, 1959), 481–92, 607.

19 See Calvin, *Institutes*, 4.17.26–33.

20 Calvin, *Institutes*, 2.13.4. On the Christology of Menno Simons (founder of the Mennonites), see Egil Grislis, "The Doctrine of Incarnation according to Menno Simons," *Journal of Mennonite Studies* 8 (1990): 16–33. Fortunately, as Grislis notes, after Simons' death the Mennonite movement returned to the Chalcedonian Christology.

21 See E. David Willis, *Calvin's Catholic Christology: The Function of the So-Called Extra Calvinisticum in Calvin's Theology* (Leiden: Brill, 1966).

22 See Edward Irving, *The Orthodox and Catholic Doctrine of Our Lord's Human Nature* (London: Baldwin and Craddock, 1830); John W. Nevin, *The Mystical Presence: A Vindication of the Reformed or Calvinistic Doctrine of the Holy Eucharist* (Philadelphia: Lippincott, 1846), 223; Thomas F. Torrance, *The Mediation of Christ* (Exeter, England: Paternoster, 1983), 48–51; and Torrance, *Incarnation*, 61–65.

23 Torrance, *Mediation of Christ*, 48–49.

24 See Torrance, *Incarnation*, 63.

25 See Bruce L. McCormack, *For Us and Our Salvation: Incarnation and Atonement in the Reformed Tradition; Studies in Reformed Theology and History*, vol. 1, no. 2 (Princeton: Princeton Theological Seminary, 1993), 17–22.

26 Calvin, *Institutes*, 1.11.8.

27 On Christ as the true image of God, see Philip Edgcumbe Hughes, *The True Image: The Origin and Destiny of Man in Christ* (Grand Rapids: Eerdmans, 1989).

28 On this cultural history of Jesus, see Jaroslav Pelikan, *Jesus through the Centuries: His Place in the History of Culture* (New Haven: Yale, 1985); and Stephen J. Nichols, *Jesus Made in America: A Cultural History from the Puritans to The Passion of the Christ* (Downers Grove, IL: InterVarsity Press, 2008).

29 Quoted in Gerald O'Collins, *Christology: A Biblical, Historical, and Systematic Study of Jesus* (New York: Oxford, 1995), 221.